CONTENTS

AUTHOR'S ACKNOWLEDGEMENTS

I am very grateful to Trish Guerri and John Simms (OTSU Ltd Senior Consultants), Brian Mee (Dyfed Open Tech) and Donald Higham (Manager, IEEIE Mathematics Open Tech Project) for penetrating and detailed comments on the first draft of this guide. I am also indebted to Don Clement (Manager, Paintmakers' Association Open Tech Project) and Clive Neville and Norman Willis (CET) for very useful suggestions. I have also been greatly encouraged by the reactions of many learners of all ages and professions, particularly Ken Mason. Finally, I am most indebted to John Coffey (CET Open Learning Unit) for useful advice and encouragement from the time when this guide was a mere idea in my mind.

Phil Race

HOW TO WIN
AS AN
OPEN LEARNER

Phil Race

 National Council for Educational Technology

Published and distributed by the
National Council for Educational Technology
3 Devonshire Street, London W1N 2BA

© Council for Educational Technology 1986

First published 1986
Reprinted 1988
Second reprint 1989
Third reprint 1991

ISBN 0 86184-165-4

NOTE: In April 1988, the National Council for Educational Technology was formed from the merger of the Microelectronics Education Support Unit with the Council for Educational Technology.

 British Library Cataloguing in Publication Data

Race, Phil
    How to win as an open learner.
    1. Study, Method of   2. Distance education
    I. Title
    371.3'028'12   LB1049

    ISBN 0-86184-165-4

Typeset by WHM Photosetting, Greenwich, SE10 8NW

Illustrations by Rosi Drew, One & A Half Graphics, Redhill

Printed in Great Britain by
BPCC Wheatons Ltd, Exeter

INTRODUCTION

CONGRATULATIONS! You're about to become an open learner. Perhaps you're already one. I'm using the word 'learner' but you may be calling yourself a student, a trainee, a client or even a customer — among other terms! However, I hope you don't mind the label 'learner', because that's the thing all customers, clients, trainees, etc have in common as soon as they dive into an open learning package — there's learning to be done. I've written this guide to help you learn.

WHAT'S THE PURPOSE OF THIS GUIDE?

Learning can be fun. Learning *should* be enjoyable. I want to help you to make your learning enjoyable by exploring with you some ideas about how you can go about it. There's another pair of words beginning with 'E' that can add up to enjoyable learning:

EFFECTIVE
EFFICIENT.

Effective is to do with getting things to stick. It's to do with helping you to retain the things you learn, rather than for them just to 'evaporate away' again. Efficient is to do with making sure you get the maximum benefit from the time you spend at your studies. If you train yourself to be really efficient, that means you don't have to spend as much time to learn a given amount — and you can enjoy the time you save in any way you like.

So if learning is effective and efficient, it will also be enjoyable because all the time you'll know you're getting good results from the time and effort you put in. Yes, effort is another word beginning with 'E', and there's no way of abolishing that one. We can make sure that your efforts are well directed, though. In this guide I hope you'll find plenty of food for thought about how to focus your efforts effectively, efficiently, and enjoyably!

WHAT SORT OF 'GUIDE' IS IT?

As it's about how to be an open learner, I've written it in an 'open' way. You'll find out more about what we mean by 'open' in Section 1 but for the moment let's look at three features of this guide that give you something to do.

1. SELF ANALYSIS QUESTIONS (SAQs)

There is one of these in each of the eight sections. Each question asks you to choose an option. The questions are similar to 'Self Assessment Questions' present in most open learning material but you'll be analysing yourself, with the help of my comments. So, every time you meet one of these questions, think carefully before you choose. Then turn to the end of the section concerned and look for the 'RESPONSES' pages. Firstly, look at what I've said in response to the option you chose. Then, it's well worth looking at the options you *didn't* choose and seeing if the reasons you rejected them match the comments I make about them in the responses to them. I know that using each SAQ in this way takes time but that's how you'll get most value out of them.

Please don't cheat! Don't read the rest of the section before you look at the responses. In many of the responses I give you further things to ponder about for a while, which are then taken up later in the text. It's no use your seeing the question when you've already explored the answer, is it?

2. OBJECTIVE CHECKLISTS

There is one of these at the end of each section, before the response to the SAQ. You might wonder why I didn't put them at the beginning of sections? Well, I want each section to be a sort of 'exploration' of various ideas and strategies. If I had set out the objectives at the beginning, the spirit of discovery would have gone.

When you come to an Objective Checklist, look at each part carefully for a moment or two, then decide whether you agree with it. When you're convinced about a part of the list (there aren't more than half a dozen in each list) maybe tick it or add your own feelings to it. Then, try to make one or two further personal objectives to add to the list. For example, you could write:

'In future, I'm going to make sure that I . . . .'

3. ACTIVITIES

There is an Activity for you to do at the end of each section. This is where you can try out some of the ideas we have been exploring in the section. Sometimes, you'll be able to enlist the help of a friend, colleague or relative to help you judge how successful your activity has been, other times you'll have a good idea of this without any help.

Many of the Activities are in bits. A bit to do straight after finishing the section, then a bit to do a few days later, perhaps.

A SUGGESTION

If you find that this guide gives you useful ideas, don't just use these ideas for a little while then forget about them (going back to old, bad habits for example!). Skim through this guide at various times in your studies. It's so easy to look at something before you start studying and say 'Ah yes, that seems a good way of doing it' then a few weeks later to have forgotten what your intentions were. Remind yourself of your intentions. The Objectives Checklists and Activities can help you to do this. Let them have their chance.

Now, over to you — and good luck with your studies.

Section 1

WHAT'S OPEN LEARNING, ANYWAY?

(The so-called experts argue about this but I'm sure you and I can agree!)

You're about to become an 'open learner', or better still, you may already have been one. However, if this is your first time, it's worth us looking at some of the differences between open learning and 'conventional' learning.

Basically, conventional learning (such as happens in classrooms and colleges) can be regarded as 'closed' in certain ways. For example, the pace is usually chosen by the teacher or lecturer. Which bit of subject is covered at any given minute is chosen by the teacher. How much detail is gone into is chosen . . . and so on. More than this, the location is fixed — the learners have to be there to take part. The time is fixed — the teacher may be angry if a learner comes in late!

Open learning programmes give as many as possible of the choices available to the learner — and now that's going to be you! Let's imagine there were such a thing as a 100 per cent 'open' programme. The learner would have control — complete control — over all sorts of decisions.

Imagine being able to decide all the following things for yourself:

Where to learn?
When to learn?
What to learn?
How fast to learn it?
How much to learn?
Whether to have your learning tested?
How to have your learning tested?
Whether to use the help of a tutor?
Whether to work with fellow learners?
Whether to do any practical or 'hands-on' work?
Whether to decide to give up learning?
Whether to bother to start at all?!

Now, I guess you'll agree with me that if you had all of these choices, it would be very easy to fall by the wayside — or even not to start at all. So most open learning programmes don't try to give you all of these responsibilities. A good open learning programme intends to leave you quite a lot of freedom to manage your own learning. This means that in many ways you're in charge. However, there is usually support and help provided for you. So, to sum up, open learning gives you more control and more responsibility. We'll look at the responsibilities in a little while, then at the advantages that come with them. Before that, however, something for you to do.

I'm calling the question that follows a 'Self Analysis Question'. It's got the initials SAQ. Most open learning materials have some sort of 'SAQs' but usually the letters stand for 'Self Assessment Question'. These are questions that get you to do something, then compare what you've done with the correct answer. In our case, I use the word 'analysis' rather than 'assessment' for a reason. My questions are to get you to think. There may not be a totally 'right' answer. So, let's stop talking about them and meet one!

SAQ 1

Why have you chosen to be an open learner, rather than use conventional methods? Tick the options that fit your reasons. Then, after making your choices, look at what I've said about each choice (not just the ones you choose yourself) at the end of the section.

I've chosen to be an *open* learner because:

(a) There is no 'conventional' course available.

(b) I can't fit a conventional course into my lifestyle or routine.

(c) I don't like conventional courses!

(d) I want to work at my own pace.

(e) My boss told me to do the course!

(f) Someone told me it was a good way to learn.

(g) (Put any other reasons of your own here):

After you've made your choice in SAQs like the one above, please turn to the end of the section and see what I've said in reply to the options you chose. It could also be useful to read my replies to the other possible choices, too.

WHAT'S THIS ABOUT RESPONSIBILITIES?

Yes, you've got them. Let's look at a few. We'll go through them one at a time, putting them in the form of questions that you'll be asking yourself from time to time.

When shall I start work as an open learner?

Answer: it's up to you! But remember it's easier to say 'tomorrow' than to dive in today. If you're ever going to start, the answer has to be 'now' on one occasion. We'll explore this business of getting started a bit more in Section 3 of this guide.

When will I do my learning?

Answer: it's up to you! It really doesn't matter when, *if* you are learning well enough. We'll take up this question in some detail in Section 3 of this guide.

Where shall I work?

Answer: it's up to you! But don't wait till you find the ideal place—you may never find it! We'll explore some possibilities in Section 4 of this guide.

I guess you get the point — the answers are all up to you! In this guide, I'll take you through all of these issues again and give a few suggestions that can make your choices a little clearer. In fact, if you look at the titles of all the sections in this book, they're all hinting at things that are ultimately up to you.

WHAT ADVANTAGES DO I GET FROM OPEN LEARNING?

Choice of pace

You can choose your *own* pace. You can go over things until you're quite confident about them. You don't need to be swamped by something before you've understood the basics that the something depends on. You can stop and go and look something up. If you're finding something easy to get to grips with, you can forge ahead at a great rate of knots. You don't have to wait for a teacher to catch up. You don't have to wait till your fellow learners catch up with you.

Choice of place

You don't have to waste time travelling to a fixed room to do your learning in. You can do much of your learning where you choose to do it.

Choice of time

You have control over when you learn. You haven't got to be tied by fixed lecture times on fixed days of fixed weeks. You can even choose to learn after everyone's gone to sleep — or maybe even before anyone's up.

Choice of method

You can enjoy privacy in your learning. What I mean is that, when you're first beginning to wrestle with something new, you needn't feel that you're going to be ridiculed for struggling. You can quietly stick at it till you've got it firmly under your belt, and then you may be ready for 'more public' scrutiny — for example sending an assignment to a tutor. If you find while studying that you need to go and look something up, you can do just that. In a live class, you may have felt you looked silly because you didn't know whatever it was. As an open learner, there's no-one to think you're silly, except occasionally yourself (but that's not a bad thing as long as you're reasonably kind to yourself!).

13

Choice of 'teacher': the learning materials

You have the advantage that the authors chosen to write most open learning courses are not just any old writers. They have to be recognised experts in their fields to be commissioned to write courses. Also, they have to be able to write. Not just a matter of writing but of composing course materials in the special way to keep you active and interested as you work on your own. Writing like this is a very demanding task. Authors have to be very careful indeed to avoid any ambiguities in their text. There's no-one to help you sort it out if something is unclear, so they have to write so as to be as understandable as possible.

This means that many open learning programmes are of a much higher quality than the average 'taught' equivalent. So as an open learner, you should be getting the best!

CHOOSING YOUR OPEN LEARNING COURSE

This isn't as easy as you may think! It would take a whole book to spell out all the various things you could take into account when making such a choice! However, I'll give a checklist of things you could try and do when making your selection.

- Check the 'prerequisites': make sure you know what you need to know to start on the materials.

- Check the objectives: make sure these fit your own needs and expectations.

- Check that there is plenty of 'interaction', such as self assessment questions for you to practise on, activities to do, practical exercises if appropriate, and so on.

- Try to find someone who has already studied using the materials concerned, and ask how it went.

- Check that all the material is readily available and not just 'in the press'! Sometimes Volume 1 is published before Volume 3 has even been written!

- Check whether there's tutorial support: this depends, of course, on whether you *want* such support.

- Check where the material is leading to: for example what can you go on to (if you wish) after you've done it?

- Last (but not least) in this short checklist, check that the material is readable. You should *enjoy* working with it and not find it hard going or boring.

OBJECTIVES CHECKLIST

Now that we've dabbled with the meaning of open learning in general terms, are you now in a better position to:

(1) Explain the ways that 'traditional' learning schemes are often 'closed' in various respects?

(2) Make a list of some of the responsibilities that fall on your shoulders as an open learner?

(3) Enjoy the advantages you have as an open learner (and recognise some of the drawbacks, which we'll try to resolve together later in this guide)?

ACTIVITY 1

Below, I've given a short list of some of the features that are present in good open learning materials. They aren't usually there in conventional textbooks. If you've already got some open learning materials (or easy access to some) have a go at this Activity. If not, please go ahead to Section 2.

Go through a few pages of your open learning materials, look for these features and decide how useful (or otherwise, of course) they will be to you personally. You can then put ticks beside the listed points below which will help you.

(1) Nice friendly tone, easy to read.

(2) Self assessment questions present, gives me the chance to try to do things.

(3) Responses to self assessment questions present. Gives me the chance to check I'm on the right track.

(4) Space for me to write my own notes on the materials.

(5) Spaces left for me to write down my answers to questions.

(6) Objectives spelled out in a useful way, helping me to see exactly what it is I'm supposed to become able to do.

(7) Useful summaries given. Helps me to see what the important things really are.

(8) Activities built in every now and then. Gives me the chance to go and apply what I'm learning.

RESPONSES TO SAQ 1

Firstly, here's the question again, to make it easier for you to see which comments go with the various options.

SAQ 1

Why have you chosen to be an open learner, rather than use conventional methods? Tick the options that fit your reasons. Then, after making your choices, look at what I've said about each choice (not just the ones you choose yourself).

I've chosen to be an *open* learner because:

(a) There is no 'conventional' course available.

(b) I can't fit a conventional course into my lifestyle or routine.

(c) I don't like conventional courses!

(d) I want to work at my own pace.

(e) My boss told me to do the course!

(f) Someone told me it was a good way to learn.

(g) Other reasons of your own.

RESPONSES

(a) 'No conventional courses available' is a good reason for choosing to be an open learner. You prove that you're not going to stop just because there isn't a ready-made pathway. You'll still need your determination, though, to keep going. Remember how much is left 'up to you' as an open learner.

(b) So you can't fit a conventional course into your lifestyle or routine. Well, that's just why many open learning routes were designed. You're in good company: plenty of very successful learners get all sorts of qualifications by open learning. Plenty of people also simply learn some new skills and many even do it for fun. If the only people to get the benefits of learning were those with easy access to conventional courses, it would be unfair on so many others.

(c) So you don't like conventional courses. Neither do I! Many people don't, sometimes because when last they were in such a course they were made to feel inferior. Adults don't like being treated like kids — neither do kids for that matter! Yet, in so many college or training courses, it happens. Now, in an open learning programme, you should find that you're treated as an adult. That does mean that you're left with various responsibilities, but more of those later.

(d) You like to work at your own pace. So do I. In conventional courses, if the pace is too fast, we get lost. If it's too slow, we get bored! It rarely seems to be just right. For most important things, it doesn't matter how fast we learn them. All that matters is how *well* we learn them and what we can do when we have learned them. A good open learning course gives you plenty of chances to see how well you're getting on. It gives you plenty of *practice* at doing the important things.

(e) So your boss told you to do it. Well, that's certainly a reason for doing it but maybe not the *best* one (the 'best' reasons are those that will help to keep you going, even when the going is a bit tough!). None of us really likes to be told to do anything! However, after a while you may find that you've got good reasons of your own for being an open learner. At least, in such a mode of study, you haven't got anyone standing over you (except perhaps that boss of yours!) telling you what to do.

(f) If someone recommended you towards open learning, you probably caught some of the enthusiasm that good open learning courses give to those who study them. I hope that you'll find yourself enjoying it so much that you'll be doing the recommending in a few months' time.

(g) I left a space for you to put reasons of your own in. Have a look at what you put (if anything) and check that they were 'good' reasons. Do this by asking yourself whether these reasons would help keep you going when things were a bit tough. If they would, they're good.

18

Section 2

WHY ARE YOU LEARNING?

(Let's make sure you have some good reasons — there'll be times when you need them!)

People learn things for all sorts of reasons. Perhaps some are better than others. I'm afraid this section is bound to overlap a bit with the previous one but it's well worth your exploring the real reasons that are leading you to doing some learning. Let's go straight into your reasons. Have a go at the following SAQ.

SAQ 2

In the previous section we looked at why you chose an open learning route for your studies. Now let's think about the more fundamental question: why are you learning at all? Choose which of the following options most closely applies to you — be honest now! Possibly more than one option fits your case, if so tick each of the relevant ones. Then look at the back of the section for my comments about the options you chose — and about the ones which you didn't.

I'm studying because:

(a) I was bored and I needed a challenge.

(b) The topic I'm studying will be useful in my job.

19

(c) Mastering the topic could lead me to promotion.

(d) Mastering the topic could lead to more choice in the jobs I could expect to get.

(e) Someone told me to study the topic concerned.

(f) I've always wanted to study this topic and now's my chance.

(g) I simply like learning new things.

(h) A friend or colleague studied it and seemed to enjoy it.

(i) I want to prove to someone that I'm better than he or she thinks I am!

(j) I want to prove to myself that I'm up to it (perhaps because I failed in it in the past).

(k) I want to be able to keep up with and help my children!

(l) I've got my own reasons (write these down here to remind you of what they are):

Now, we've looked at a number of possible reasons for studying. There are probably as many different reasons as there are learners — and we're all learners! Don't worry that some of my responses to the options in the SAQ ended on something of a 'warning' note; I wanted to get you thinking about how your reasons for learning would stand up to pressure. You'll have seen from my responses to the options you chose in the SAQ how well your reasons are going to serve you. You may even have found some new and better reasons for learning. If so, I'm glad.

The fact remains that we need reasons for doing demanding things like studying. The more reasons the better. When things get a bit tough, these reasons can be the driving force that keeps us on course. Let's face it, it's bound to be tough now and then — anything worthwhile is. Imagine if universities gave all students who lived there for three years a degree, no matter how little they worked. A degree would be quite worthless. There wouldn't be any point in working for one.

Ultimately, the only person who can assess how good your reasons for learning are now — is yourself. That's why I'm not going to say any more apart from the comments I made in the responses to the SAQ. If I have helped you to reappraise your motives, well and good!

OBJECTIVES CHECKLIST

Now that you've 'psychoanalysed' your motives, you could now be sadder (surely not!), wiser (of course!) and more likely to keep your nose to the grindstone. Are you now in a position to:

(1) Recite some good reasons for sticking to your studies, convincingly enough to keep you at them even on those dark days we all get from time to time?

(2) Feel a sense of purpose in what you are doing?

(3) Abandon any 'bad' reasons you might have had (or at least turn them into better reasons)?

ACTIVITY 2

Now that we've been through various good, and some not-so-good, reasons for studying, take a small piece of paper or card and write down the reasons you personally have ended up with — those that will stand the tests of time and circumstance. Stick your list up somewhere where you will see it every day. Whether you choose a 'public' or a 'private' site for your list will depend whether your reasons are ones that you can share with friends or relatives; that doesn't matter. The main thing is that *your* reasons should keep *you* going.

RESPONSES TO SAQ 2

First, another look at the question.

SAQ 2

In the previous section we looked at why you chose an open learning route for your studies. Now let's think about the more fundamental question: why are you learning at all? Choose which of the following options most closely applies to you — be honest now! Possibly more than one option fits your case, if so tick each of the relevant ones. Then look below for my comments about the options you chose — and about the ones which you didn't.

I'm studying because:

(a) I was bored and I needed a challenge.

(b) The topic I'm studying will be useful in my job.

(c) Mastering the topic could lead me to promotion.

(d) Mastering the topic could lead to more choice in the jobs I could expect to get.

(e) Someone told me to study the topic concerned.

(f) I've always wanted to study this topic and now's my chance.

(g) I simply like learning new things.

(h) A friend or colleague studied it and seemed to enjoy it.

(i) I want to prove to someone that I'm better than he or she thinks I am!

(j) I want to prove to myself that I'm up to it (perhaps because I failed in it in the past).

(k) I want to be able to keep up with and help my children!

(l) I've got my own reasons (write these down to remind you of what they are).

RESPONSES

(a) You say you're studying because you were bored and needed a challenge. An interesting reason. Studying is certainly a way of finding challenges and if you were bored you are likely to have sufficient time available to study. However, suppose something else came up that was more interesting. Would that mean that when you were no longer bored, you'd abandon your studies?

(b) So the subject you're studying will be useful in your job. That's a good reason for studying. It gives you a sense of purpose which will be helpful at those times when the studying gets a bit hard. Also, when you can apply the things you study, you get more satisfaction than if you were just studying something in theory without having any chances to put it into practice.

(c) You say you're studying to increase your chances of promotion. That certainly can be a powerful incentive. It's probably one of the commonest reasons that people endure quite taxing programmes of study. But let's look at two possibilities: firstly, if after studying you didn't get promotion, how would you feel? Cheated? Let down? A feeling of having wasted your time studying? Or would it have been worthwhile anyway? Secondly, suppose you got promoted halfway through your studies. Would you then stop studying because you no longer needed to? So you see there are dangers associated with this reason for studying, particularly if it's your *only* reason for studying.

(d) You're studying to widen the range of jobs you might get. This is actually a very good reason. Psychologists tell us that every few years we should change our career directions. This stops us getting stale and set in our ways. It makes life more interesting and satisfying. I'm not saying it makes life easier — it's often easier to continue to do what one was doing. However, the more choices you have in what you do, the greater the chance that you can choose to do something that you really like. Job satisfaction is so much more important than what you're paid. If you have more choices available, the chance of selecting a well paid job is bound to increase but, more importantly, you should be able to select a really satisfying job as well.

(e) So someone told you to study. Maybe your employer. Does this mean you're only doing it because you have to? Does this in turn mean that you rather resent having to? None of us likes to be told to do something. The danger is that if you've got resentful feelings, every little obstacle you come across will seem like a mountain and you may not feel like giving of your best when things are a bit tough. If this is your only reason for studying, it may be worth your trying to find some additional reasons of your own.

(f)   You say you've always wanted to study the topic concerned and now are taking your chance. That's a fine reason. Many people make this reason work for them. But what would happen if, when you get a bit deeper into the subject, you find it a lot harder than you expected? Just about everything is easy at first but gets tougher when you go deeper into it. The worst thing that could happen is that you'd sail along while the going was easy but get fed up with the topic when it got a bit harder. So, you really need to try to build some extra reasons to help keep you going.

(g)   You like learning new things, do you? It's a good reason for studying, as long as you're prepared to keep going when the going is tough (as it's bound to be at times in any worthwhile programme of study).

(h)   You're following the recommendation of a friend or colleague, I see. This can be very useful because it means that someone has already found the course valuable and interesting. Not all open learning courses can claim to be that! Check, though, that you're not just doing the course to prove you're as good as your friend or colleague. It might be worth asking what your friend's reasons were for doing the course and also asking whether these reasons helped keep your friend going when things weren't too easy.

(i)   You want to prove to someone that you're better than he or she thinks! Well, at least you're being honest. But does it really matter that much what people think about you? What really matters is what you think of yourself. It would be useful if you had reasons for studying that were useful to you and nothing to do with anyone else.

(j)   Wanting to prove to yourself that you can do a thing is a strong reason for doing it. If you've maybe been successful at something in the past, it is certainly a nice experience to prove yourself up to it now. But don't be too hard on yourself. It's even more important to *enjoy* your studies. That way your success will be all the more certain.

(k) Well done! Wishing to be able to keep up with, and help, your children in their studies is a healthy reason for you to do some studying of your own. Besides, when children see parents studying, they form the useful impression that studying is a perfectly normal part of life.

(l) So you have reasons of your own. The main thing for you to check is that they are reasons that will keep you going through rough and smooth. Only you can check this!

Section 3

WHEN WILL YOU LEARN?

(I, too, could do with a 30-hour day sometimes!)

Learning takes time! That's obvious enough. The problem is finding the time. You probably had a full and busy life before you decided to do some open learning — I doubt if you found yourself twiddling your thumbs! All the things that kept you busy before will still be around — they don't magically disappear just because you're now going to do some studying. Actually, finding the time to learn is only part way towards successful learning. What is even more important is being able to make the most effective use of what time you can find. That's where I hope to help you — not only in this section but throughout this guide. Let's see what your intentions look like.

SAQ 3

How do you see yourself timetabling your study patterns? Which of the following is closest to your way of doing things? (Or what strategy do you intend to adopt?)

(a) I like to plan a nice tight schedule, for example: Mondays, 7.15-9.00 pm, Wednesdays, . . . etc.

(b) I tend to work in bursts when the mood takes me. I don't like the idea of regimenting my study times!

(c) I've got a busy week, so I'll have to study at weekends. I expect I'll be able to fit one or two long spells of study into most weekends.

(d) I'll study whenever there's nothing else crying out to be done.

(e) I do quite a bit of travelling. I expect I'll be able to fit some studying into my journeys.

(f) None of the above fits me. The way I'll work is as follows (jot it down please):

HOW LONG DOES IT TAKE TO DO SOME STUDYING?

Two hours? Half a day? I prefer the answer to be in minutes! A small number of minutes in fact! It's surprising what we can learn in a very short time. It's equally surprising how little we sometimes learn, given a long spell of studying. What happens? Do you know what I mean by 'drifting'? One can sit at a desk, hour after hour, with the regular sound of pages being turned, with very little real work happening! Has this happened to you? You might as well have been enjoying yourself doing something else, rather than sitting for hours kidding yourself you were working. The danger is particularly bad when reading. Reading can so easily be a very passive activity. Enjoyable it may be but to be useful it has to be made active. More of that later in this guide.

So, our minds seem to do the *real* work in quite short bursts. Perhaps about an hour may be the *most* that our minds can really concentrate on so demanding a task as learning something new (my mind manages about 20 minutes!). Our brains rebel or switch off if we try to make them concentrate for a long time. Then, putting off starting some study until a suitable two-hour spell is available is not such a splendid idea. In fact, waiting for a suitably long spell to become available is really often just an *excuse* to put off the moment of starting to study! There's always something useful you can do in a few minutes. True, you can't learn Einstein's theory of relativity in a few minutes but you can always check through something you've already learned and make sure it's still 'there'.

There are certainly some advantages to having a regular study routine — as long as the routine doesn't become too rigid. If it's rigid, sooner or later you'll rebel against it and then feel a sense of failure. You could feel that you haven't lived up to your expectations. To avoid this happening, your routine needs to be able to allow you to work more when you have time to spare or are particularly enthusiastic about the topic you're studying. The routine also needs to allow you to work less when you have other crises to deal with. The key ingredient in a routine you can live with is *flexibility*. For example, you could plan half a dozen study periods in a week, with the proviso that you want, on average, to use four of them each week. When you really feel like studying, you could use all six. You could earn yourself some time off in advance when you knew next week was going to have more pressures on you and less time for study.

Remembering the shortness of our average concentration span, each study period needs to have variety built in to it. A change is as good as a rest. We'll explore the ways you can build in changes later in this guide. The study periods themselves can be kept short. A lot of short bursts of activity tend to work better than a few rather boring long ones. It's much easier to fit short spells of studying into a busy lifestyle anyway.

WHAT ABOUT ALL THOSE OTHER JOBS?

'No, I can't start learning today, I've simply got to . . . . first'.

'I'll do some learning after I've got . . . . out of the way'.

Be honest, there are always going to be things you can use for the

'. . . .'. Possibly some of these things have been waiting for a long time to get done. Sometimes they may be urgent. Suppose you had an urgent job that had to be done by tomorrow; let's say it would take two hours, for the sake of argument. Let's look at three ways of dealing with it.

A: Do the urgent job, leave studying till another day.

B: Do the urgent job, and fit in say half an hour of study after it's done.

C: Do half an hour's worth of study, then do the urgent job.

Well, you can see what's wrong with A. It is possible to put off studying indefinitely that way! B is more dangerous. What if the job takes more than two hours? Goodbye, studying. Even if the urgent job gets done easily enough, will you really honour your intention to get that half hour in afterwards? You may be tired or another urgent job might have come up meanwhile! How about C?

It takes a bit of courage to postpone the urgent job for a while. But the studying *does get done*! And what about the urgent job? Well, that gets done too — after all it *has* to get done by tomorrow. And you've got the advantage of studying while you're fresh, rather than when you are tired after doing the urgent job.

So, a useful policy is:

'Do a bit of studying *before* whatever else you simply must do.'

It's surprising how quickly these bits of studying add up to something very worthwhile. In fact, many of the so-called urgent jobs turn out to be *excuses* for not starting studying! By doing the studying first, you don't let yourself be cheated by them. You actually use the urgent jobs to help you study because, before you start on each such job, you put in a bit of studying! Simple, isn't it? You probably agree with me at the moment but will you put the idea into practice? The choice is yours — no-one can force you. As an open learner, you're free to choose whichever way to learn (including the hard ways!) any time you wish!

EVEN ODDER BITS OF TIME!

Let me tell you a true story. When I was first at college, I had a 40 minute bus journey each way. One of my subjects was Chemical Kinetics. There happened to be a good, pocket-sized textbook on that subject. Somehow, I got into the habit of letting that book live in my jacket pocket. On every journey — no, I *didn't* read the book for 40 minutes! What I did was to look at something in it for maybe a couple of minutes. Then I'd put it away again and continue reading everyone else's newspapers!

Anyway, after two terms came the exams. I sat down to start to learn Chemical Kinetics and found that I already knew it well. I could 'think' myself up on to the top deck of the bus and see diagrams, derivations and explanations in my mind's eye. It would probably have taken me at least 30 hours to learn the subject from scratch and I'd saved myself all that time just by a couple of minutes here and there — *regularly*. Have you any such odd bits of time? You're bound to have. The secret is to have something with you that you can do during those odd minutes. It doesn't have to be a book. Something written on a postcard would do. There's a saying, 'if you want a good job done, give it to a busy person'. Could it be that such people have mastered the art of using odd bits of time? I think so.

31

OBJECTIVES CHECKLIST

Now that we've explored the question of 'When will you learn', are you now able to:

(1) Agree that all your best reasons regarding when you *can't* learn have been excuses!?

(2) Adopt a studying regime that matches your personality — one you can stick to?

(3) Maximise the usefulness of odd bits of time?

(4) Realise that the *real* question isn't 'am I studying for long enough' but is 'am I doing sufficient useful work'? (In Section 5 we'll explore how you can answer this question.)

ACTIVITY 3

(1) Set yourself a target for the total number of study-hours that you intend to put in, in the week beginning now.

(2) Prepare a sheet of paper to log in time actually spent studying. (Don't include any time you indulge in *thinking* about starting to work!)

(3) After the week is up, decide:

   (a) was the target a realistic one?

   (b) did you meet it (or exceed it)?

   (c) did the fact you were keeping a log help make sure you did your studying?

   (d) would it be useful to continue to log the time you spend studying?

32

RESPONSES TO SAQ 3

As usual, a reminder of the question.

SAQ 3

How do you see yourself timetabling your study patterns? Which of the following is closest to your way of doing things? (Or what strategy do you intend to adopt?)

(a) I like to plan a nice tight schedule, for example: Mondays, 7.15-9.00 pm, Wednesdays, . . . etc.

(b) I tend to work in bursts when the mood takes me. I don't like the idea of regimenting my study times!

(c) I've got a busy week, so I'll have to study at weekends. I expect I'll be able to fit one or two long spells of study into most weekends.

(d) I'll study whenever there's nothing else crying out to be done.

(e) I do quite a bit of travelling. I expect I'll be able to fit some studying into my journeys.

(f) None of the above fits me. The way I'll work is as follows.

RESPONSES

(a) So you like working to a nice tight schedule. Congratulations if you're someone who has made this work for you in the past. It takes a lot of self discipline. Can I ask you one or two rather painful questions, however?

> Do you sometimes catch yourself thinking about all sorts of other things during your planned study sessions?

> Are you sure that you can maintain your efficiency even when other things are on your mind?

It's good to have a tight schedule if you find that you *enjoy* working that way, even when the going is a bit tough. But, a last question:

> Might there be lots of other useful times when you could be doing a bit of study, when you don't try simply because they're not on your schedule?

A schedule can become an excuse to do *nothing* in all the unscheduled times!

(b) You work in bursts when the mood takes you, you say? And you don't like being regimented? This is, of course, fine so long as enough work is getting done, steadily and surely. After all, we're talking about open learning, you're in charge of the times and pace.

Now, when things are going well and you're full of enthusiasm, you'll obviously get a lot of work done this way. Probably you'll do much more than you would have if you'd been working to a schedule. But what happens when the going gets a bit tough? What if your enthusiasm temporarily deserts you? Does this mean you might simply stop in your tracks? Would some sort of schedule help then, or is there a better way?

(c) Many open learners have busy weeks and work at weekends. It seems a fact of life that weekends are regarded as the time when miracles are possible! I once wrote for an editor who always set deadlines for receiving manuscript on Tuesdays because he knew very well that most authors get behind schedule and make desperate attempts to catch up during the last available weekend, so the manuscript would be in the post Monday morning and (with luck!!) would be on his desk on Tuesday. The trouble with *only* working at weekends is that studying doesn't quite become a full part of one's life. A lot can be forgotten from one weekend to the next. Also, families and friends can feel neglected if there's no time for them at weekends.

(d) So you'll do some studying whenever there's nothing else crying out to be done. Well done for being prepared to study anytime and not just in scheduled bursts or during weekends. But be honest, there are always going to be other things needing doing. Maybe they've needed doing for months. Could you say there's been a time when you'd completely caught up with everything? Now, the real danger is that when the studying gets a bit difficult, all those other things suddenly seem more attractive and more urgent! I'm sure there are plenty of ceilings that got painted as a refuge from a bit of hard studying!

(e) So you do quite a bit of travelling? So do I. I too manage to do quite a bit of work, especially on trains. Perhaps British Rail coffee makes me more efficient? I'll be saying more about this method of studying in Section 4.

(f) You claimed that none of the options fitted you and you had plans of your own. If you've read through the responses above, perhaps you'll agree with my comments about the dangers (and the advantages) of the various options discussed. How do these comments fit your way of studying? The real questions to ask yourself about your method are:

Will I make best use of my available time?

Will enough useful work get done, steadily?

Will my method continue to work when other important things crop up in my life?

35

Section 4

WHERE WILL YOU LEARN?

(Have you already got yourself an executive-style study?)

I often ask college-based students this question. After all, not much of the real learning happens during class-time. Students need to do a lot of work on their own. If I ask the question of a large group of students, you can bet that their answers will be roughly like this: some will say 'in my bedroom'; others will say 'in the library'; many will say 'at home, on the dining room table'; some will say 'wherever I can'.

Now, you're an open learner. You won't have the sort of study-bedroom that some college students have (those, that is, who are lucky enough to get into halls of residence). You probably won't have the same sort of access to a library. At least, it could be difficult to carry all your learning materials in and out of your local library any time you choose. So, let's see how you're fixed regarding where you'll be studying.

SAQ 4

Which of the following is nearest to your situation regarding where you'll be doing most of your learning?

(a) I'll have to sort out a suitable study area at home.

(b) I've no problem, I've already got a good place for studying at home.

(c) I'll have to go out to study, maybe to a library or some such place.

(d) I'll be doing much of my studying at work, where I have a suitable place.

(e) I've got a garden shed! Are you suggesting that I turn this into a study?

(f) Help!! I really don't know where I'm going to find space to do my learning.

SORTING OUT THE BITS AND PIECES

Suppose you have somewhere to study (it doesn't matter where for the moment). Imagine you've just arrived at your desk or table and you're going to do some studying — let's say for an hour or so. How do you start?

Perhaps you tidy up the table a bit first. Then maybe you get together all the learning materials you may be using, and pens and paper. Maybe you'll need a calculator or some drawing instruments, so out they come. Then, perhaps, you get a cup of coffee on to the front right-hand corner of the desk, to sustain you during your efforts. Maybe next, you put the radio or cassette player on the back of the desk and get a suitable background sound going. You'll need oxygen during your studies, so perhaps you open the window a bit. Then, because the air coming in is rather cool, you adjust the heating. On your way back to the desk, you notice that you haven't cleaned your shoes for a few weeks and rectify that.

See what I'm getting at? Have you caught yourself spending ages rearranging your environment before getting down to some real work? Believe me, I've caught myself. I can assure you it is

38

perfectly possible to postpone the real work for the whole hour —
maybe for weeks!

Why do we do things like this? Is it because we have to get our
minds 'in gear' ready for that dreaded moment of actually starting
work? I think we sort out the bits and pieces because all these other
activities are *easier* than actually doing some work. They are
excuses for not starting.

I now try to do as follows. Even if my desk is cluttered (it usually is),
I push back the clutter to make enough room for what I'm about to
read. We can only read one thing at a time. I make room for the
paper I'm going to write on, pick up a pen and *start*! I'll work for
maybe ten minutes or so. Then I'll stop and see whether I still think
it's urgent to tidy up the desk — usually it isn't. Usually I'm by now
absorbed with what I'm studying. Even when I do decide to tidy up
the desk, the things I've been working with for the ten minutes will
be going through my mind. We all need time to ponder things.
No-one can concentrate for long periods. So now and then I take a
few minutes off and tidy up, get the coffee, tune the radio, adjust
the heating and so on.

SO WHERE IS THE BEST
PLACE TO STUDY?

Think back to the responses to the options in the SAQ. I made
cautionary comments about most kinds of places for studying.
There's an even more important danger.

Imagine you have got an excellent place (home, work, wherever) —
somewhere that really suits you. You study efficiently there. What
happens when you're *not* there? Do you use the fact that you're
not in your ideal place as a reason not to bother trying to study? 'I'll
wait till I get back to where I can really make progress' you might
say. Is that a reason? *It's an excuse!*

My advice is to become able to do a bit of studying almost
wherever you are. Make studying a real part of your whole life, not

just something that happens in a particular room. That said, there are advantages in having a 'safe' area for studying — an area that family and friends will recognise as a 'please don't disturb me here' place.

Am I suggesting that you carry around all your learning materials with you all over the place? No, I'm not. All you need with you is 'something' related to your studies. Later in this guide we'll go into what the 'something' can be. You'll find that there are many possibilities. If the 'something' is small and pocketable, the more likely it is that you'll use it during those odd few minutes. You'll become more able to do useful little bits of studying even in the oddest places!

WORKING IN ODD PLACES!

Let's imagine there's one vital bit of information you really have to learn well. It may only take five minutes to do it. It's night and it's raining outside. Imagine you do this (don't do it, just think about it!): pick up a flashlight and an umbrella, go outside with the bit you're going to learn, spend five minutes learning it, then come back in. (Never mind the neighbours!) Now my guess is that you'd *remember* that bit of learning very efficiently. Simply because you'd done something so different, it would stick in your mind.

That might have been an extreme example but do you see the principle involved? It's to do with 'association'. If you can 'hook up' the thing you're wanting to remember to something else memorable, it's much easier to recall the thing concerned. Obviously, I'm not suggesting that you do all of your learning in unusual places. But, if you have something with you and a few spare minutes, there's no reason for not doing a bit wherever you are, when the mood takes you. If you didn't have something with you, you wouldn't have the choice of doing a bit. In fact, then you'd have a reason for *not* doing anything. No, an *excuse*!!

OBJECTIVES CHECKLIST

Now that we've abandoned the search for a learner's paradise, are you ready to:

(1) Make the most of the various learning environments available to you?

(2) Explore what can be done with 'unlikely' learning environments?

(3) Start learning straight away, rather than do a lot of sorting out first?

(4) Blend your studies into the whole of your lifestyle, rather than confining them to a 'tidy corner' of your life?

ACTIVITY 4

(1) Make a plan to study for let's say a quarter of an hour in each of three places you've not used before for studying. Stick to your plan and see how it goes in the three places.

(2) After a week or two, spend five minutes just thinking back to what you learned in those three places. Decide for yourself whether any or all of the different environments helped you to remember what you learned on those three occasions.

(3) (Optional!) If you happen to be in a position to observe a friend or colleague studying (no matter what), see whether he or she wastes time 'sorting out the bits and pieces' before really getting started. If so, tell the person concerned about it — or decide you'd better not mention it! (No-one likes being found out!)

RESPONSES TO SAQ 4

So where will you be working? The options I gave you are repeated below.

SAQ 4

Which of the following is nearest to your situation regarding where you'll be doing most of your learning?

(a) I'll have to sort out a suitable study area at home.

(b) I've no problem, I've already got a good place for studying at home.

(c) I'll have to go out to study, maybe to a library or some such place.

(d) I'll be doing much of my studying at work, where I have a suitable place.

(e) I've got a garden shed! Are you suggesting that I turn this into a study?

(f) Help!! I really don't know where I'm going to find space to do my learning.

RESPONSES

(a) You're in good company. Most open learners when first starting to study this way need to sort out something at home. But be careful! It's possible to spend a long time sorting out things at home, rather than actually getting some learning under way. Remember the dangers of 'all those other urgent jobs'?

(b) Congratulations, you already have a good study base at home, you say. Even so, there are dangers to be avoided. Will your place at home be the *only* place you'll use for studying?

(c) So you intend to go out to a suitable place (maybe a library) to do most of your studying. True, when you get there you may indeed work efficiently. But will you actually get there when there's a force eight blowing, or a foot of snow, or if you've got a bit of a cough?

(d) You say you have facilities for study at work. So do I. My room even has such luxuries as a phone, a light and a door! And I have a key to the building, so I can go there anytime. It's only five minutes' walk from where I live too. But what happens? When I study there during the day, the phone rings. It's easier chatting on the phone than studying! And the door keeps opening and colleagues come up and say 'Oh, what are you up to now?' and it's more relaxing to tell them all about it than to continue doing some studying. Of course, I can go along when the place is almost deserted. But that's where my light comes in. When the security man notices it, he comes along to see if it has been left on by mistake. Soon we're happily chatting about what I'm doing, or should I say *not* doing! So, though I often study at my workplace, it certainly isn't the only place I use.

(e) I envy you! I haven't a shed. I haven't a garden, in fact, and I miss gardening. I do have a small yard but my wife won't let me put up a shed! She knows I'd lurk in it and be unavailable when jobs needed doing! A shed could serve as a study, away from many of the distractions that abound in homes. But it would have to be a comfortable shed, wouldn't it? It would need some mod cons like coffee-making facilities, heat, and so on.

(f) So you don't know yet what to do about a good place to study. Well, if you've read the rest of the responses I gave above, you'll have noticed that even the best places have problems associated with them. In fact, it's more useful if you can do some studying in less-than-ideal circumstances, than to search endlessly for the ideal place. What's even more important is that you study efficiently — more of that later in this guide. It's only too easy to sit in the best study in the world and daydream!

Section 5

HOW WILL YOU MAKE YOUR LEARNING REALLY EFFICIENT?

('Enjoyment got through studying is proportional to the square of your efficiency' — Phil's First Law!)

We've already noticed that it's possible to sit at a desk (or anywhere else) trying to learn, even pretending to learn. It's possible to have been trying for hours and for nothing much to have happened. We're now going to find ways of stopping such wastage of your time. We'll look at ways of getting things to stick.

Is your memory not what you'd like it to be? Try this. Think of a meal you had yesterday — say the main one of the day. Suppose I asked you to write down everything about that meal. Think about it for one minute now (don't write it but do stop for that minute and think).

What went through your mind? You could have thought in that minute of all sorts of things. Here are some:

    what you ate
    whether it was good or not
    whether it was hot or cold
    what colours the food was
    the place where you were eating
    who else was there
    what you said
    what anyone else said
    what you thought of what they said

what was on your mind as you ate
what you were going to do next
and so on, all sorts of related things.

Now, I bet if you wrote all this down, you could have filled several pages. But no-one asked you to remember all this, yet you did. Your memory is all right, isn't it? Perhaps the way you *use* it can be polished up. We'll see what we can do soon. What am I getting at by the word 'efficiency' then? See what you think.

SAQ 5

Which one of the following do you reckon is most closely connected with studying efficiently?

(a) Knowing that I'm spending plenty of time studying.

(b) Having the feeling that I know the subject well after I've studied it for a while.

(c) Having done plenty of practice at answering questions on the subject.

BUILDING IN ACTIVITY

The thing to avoid is wasting time in passive study. There are several things you can do to keep active. To be active you've got to keep getting yourself in the 'decision-making' mode — when making decisions you can't really remain passive. Let's explore some ways of doing this.

Answering questions

Your learning materials probably have lots of questions for you to try yourself out on. They may be called 'Self Assessment Questions' or SAQs. (Notice that mine in this guide are concerned with self *analysis*, in other words questions that give you a chance of exploring your own study habits and attitudes; they are still, of course, self assessment questions at the same time.)

Where your materials contain SAQs, or whatever the material designers chose to call them, there should be *responses* for you to look at after doing the question, so you can see how you did. The responses may help you spot common mistakes, and give you ideas about avoiding them.

Now, every time you meet an SAQ, you have several choices. These include:

(1) Doing exactly what the question asks you to, *then* looking at the answer or response given in the materials, and *deciding* how well you did.

(2) *Thinking* how you would answer the question (without actually *doing* it) then turning to the response to see if your thoughts had been on the right lines.

(3) Skipping the question and reading on (this is tempting, especially if you're dying to find out what's coming next).

Now look back at those three choices (and there are more I've not mentioned) and look for the only good choice. Yes, it's the first one. It takes a bit of discipline but it's worth it. Choice number (2) really isn't as good because you won't *remember* what you were thinking (be it right or wrong) for very long after you've looked at the response. For example, you may have been thinking wrongly and as soon as you see the response you say to yourself 'of course, now I see'. But you'll not remember the wrong thinking to avoid in future for nearly as long as if you'd committed yourself and checked your full answer against the response given in the materials. Choice number (3) is all too easy but if you make that choice, you're deciding to be passive rather than active. You'd miss out on all the practice the designers of the learning materials carefully built in for you.

'But if I *know* that my answer is right, why bother writing it down or checking with the response?' It's still worth the short time it would take to put down your answer in writing, it's useful practice. You may know something in an exam but you've still got to express it on paper before you get any credit for it.

To sum up on SAQs and suchlike, it's worth treating them seriously and not depriving yourself of the practice they give you. Also, it's worth using them as periodic revision tests, to see if any of the things you could do have 'slipped'. It's very useful indeed to discover just which bits are prone to slip because then (and only then) you can do something about them and you can practice with them.

Making learning tools
Firstly, how about a *'question bank'*?

Imagine you had a collection of all the questions that you could possibly have to answer to prove that you knew a topic. Imagine next that you'd practised with this collection till you could answer the lot! Well, you'd know the topic of course. What's more, you'd be able to prove to anyone (yourself, an examiner, anyone at all) that you knew it. Let's call this collection of questions a question bank. Any exam question (past or future) would be contained in the collection. That doesn't mean the question bank is a huge collection of exam questions. It's a collection of all the little questions that make up such bigger questions. It's all the things you need to become able to do *do, make, draw, describe, explain* . . . All those active words again.

The question bank questions should be short and direct. It only takes seconds to write one. How do you decide what questions to write? You'll soon develop the skill if you do as follows.

Think for a minute about the following question (recite it a few times if you like):

'What am I expected to be able to do?'

This is the most important question to have in your mind all the time you're studying. But rather than write down answers to this question, write *short, sharp questions* for yourself to practise on. Suppose you've been studying a couple of pages of learning material. Ask that question about the material and turn your replies into a set of short questions — it could look something like this:

Sketch a . . . .
Define the word . . . .
Describe a . . . .
List 5 features of a . . . .
State . . . .'s Law
How many . . . .s in a . . . .?
Why does . . . . happen?
When does . . . . happen?
How does a . . . . work?

The variety of these little questions is endless. But, if you can answer them all, you know the topic — and you *know* you do. A nice feeling — and a deserved one.

Let's go back again to the big question (what am I expected to be able to do?) and look at one word in it, the word *expected*. That's important. You could, of course, write yourself little questions on things no-one expected you to become able to do. There's no point doing that. So when you can tell that there's no *need* for you to do something, you don't include the question on that something in your question bank. This could happen when your learning materials are doing some of the following (and many similar things you'll be able to decide):

Setting the scene.

Going into details that no-one would need to remember word-for-word or number-for-number, and so on.

So all the time you have these decisions to make:

(1) Is it important enough to write a question bank entry about?

(2) *What am I expected to be able to do?*

(3) How can I turn what I *am* expected to become able to do into questions for me to practise on?

'All this decision making!' you may be saying. But they're actually quite easy decisions in practice and they *keep you active*. What's even more important is that you get something to show for your efforts. That list of questions you build up as you study is a *learning tool*. It's something you can practise with. It's something you can use to measure how well you're doing.

It's one of those 'somethings' I mentioned in the last section, things you can carry around with you. Suppose you wrote your sets of short questions on cards or in a pocket notebook. You could take a card (or a page) wherever you were, quickly look at each question in turn and *decide* whether you could still answer it. You could maybe tick it if you knew you could answer it. You could maybe cross it if you couldn't answer it. So what have you gained? A lot. You've quickly thought through a lot of things you can still do (a lot quicker than reading the original learning material sections).

But more important, you've found out which bits you can't do at the moment. You know now what will need a bit more practice or what needs looking up in more detail. And the question bank is intact, a tool ready for you to use again and again. You can continue to add to it every time you recognise something else you may be expected to become able to do.

Tools that aren't used go rusty. So make sure that you do use your question bank — it only takes minutes to go through a bit of it, checking. Whenever you work with it, whether adding to it as you study or practising with it, you can rest assured you'll automatically be learning actively because you'll be keeping yourself in decision-making mode. How much more efficient this sort of approach is compared to just passively reading.

We've spent quite some time on that first sort of learning tool, the question bank. But there's another kind of useful activity I'd like you to think about. I'll get straight to the point this time: it's *making summaries*. Suppose you spend 15 minutes making a summary of all the main points in a few pages of material. Once again, you are being active. Again, you're making decisions all the time. You're judging what's important. You're judging what is mere background detail (and, of course, missing such things out of your summary).

What uses can summaries have? Of course, they too are *learning tools*. They're something tangible to show for your efforts. They're compact and concise, so you can carry them around with you. You can use them to revise main points. You can spend the odd five minutes here and there refreshing your grasp of something by thinking through your summary. You can use your summary to help you with those question bank questions that have slipped.

I haven't said as much about summaries as I did about question banks. That's simply because the idea of making summaries is familiar to many people, whereas my question bank method is not. Both sorts of learning tool are very useful. Making and using both ensure that studying is an active process — an *efficient* process.

OBJECTIVES CHECKLIST

Now that we've explored some aspects of making studying efficient, I trust that your personal strategy will include the following ideas and practices.

(1) Working efficiently is far more important than simply spending a lot of hours studying. It may mean you can get a lot more done in a much shorter number of hours.

(2) Efficiency can best be measured by your ability to answer questions and do things — and by the *speed* you develop.

(3) Efficiency in studying can be dramatically improved by giving yourself practice at answering questions.

(4) You can make the tools to increase your efficiency bit by bit as you study by making question banks and summaries.

(5) It's well worth using to the full those questions and activities already built into your learning materials. You can add things asked in SAQs, for example, to your own (much fuller) question bank.

(6) Now that you know how learning can be made more efficient by keeping it active and by staying in decision-making mode, the next decision is yours to take: whether to take heed of the things we've been exploring (or whether to be passive — no-one will stop you from studying this way if you choose to!).

ACTIVITY 5

This activity is intended to give you the chance to find out how useful it is to use my question bank principles.

(1) Choose a few pages of material you want to get to grips with. (If you've not yet started your open learning course, choose something you've learned in this guide or something that relates to what you're going to study soon.)

(2) Work through your chosen material, writing short, sharp questions whenever you feel you may be expected to be able to remember or do something. Try to get between 10 and 20 questions.

(3) After a week or so, look at your questions without looking at the original materials. Tick the questions you're sure you can still do and put crosses beside the ones you know you can't do (and maybe an asterisk beside those you're not sure whether you can still answer or not). Then look up the answers again for the ones which you can't do.

(4) After another week or so, see how many of the 'crossed' questions on your list you can still answer. If there are some you can't, look up the answers once more and this time design some 'clues' which you can add beside the questions.

(5) Continue going back to your list of questions every now and then, until you can answer them all every time you try it.

Don't worry at all if certain questions prove particularly elusive. It's of great value simply to find out which these questions are. Then you're well on the way towards cracking the problem. You know where to practise that bit more.

RESPONSES TO SAQ 5

Once again, another look at the question.

SAQ 5
Which one of the following do you reckon is most closely connected with studying efficiently?

(a) Knowing that I'm spending plenty of time studying.

(b) Having the feeling that I know the subject well after I've studied it for a while.

(c) Having done plenty of practice at answering questions on the subject.

RESPONSES
(a) It's good to know you are spending plenty of time at your studies but that's not a guarantee that you're using that time efficiently. Maybe you could achieve twice as much in half the time? Maybe you could then afford much more time off doing the other things that make up your life? Time can be deceptive. There's no substitute for practising answering questions and practising doing things.

(b) It's a comfortable feeling when you feel you know a topic well after you've worked with it for a while. But how can you tell you really do know it well? Feelings can be deceptive. What we really need is a way for you to prove to yourself (and anyone else for that matter) how well you know the topic. That means showing your knowledge by being able to *do* things, *answer* questions, *make* deductions, *explain* things, *describe* things, maybe *calculate* things, maybe *draw* things, maybe *discuss* things or *interpret* things — I'm sure you can think of lots of such activities. All the words in italics in the last sentence have one thing in common: they are the active words in questions (can you think of any exam question, for example, that hasn't one such word in it?). Now, if you'd been doing a lot of practice at answering questions, you'd *know* that you knew the topic well because you'd have proved to yourself that you did. But then you would have chosen option (c), wouldn't you?

(c) I agree with you, this is by far the happiest answer to SAQ 5. It's only when you've been doing a lot of practice at answering questions or doing things with your topic that you can tell how well you're getting on. *Feeling* that you're doing great isn't enough on its own. Knowing that you've put a lot of time in isn't enough either. The real pleasure comes from 'getting the answers right' and being able to recall them later.

If you look back to my response for option (b) above, you'll notice I picked out some 'active' words like *do, draw, describe, discuss, make* and so on. It's worth you making your own list of the similar words that relate to your particular subjects. If you were learning to drive a car, some such words could be *start* the car, *change* gear, *judge* distances, *choose* the best speed, *steer* properly. People who couldn't do those things certainly couldn't drive well (though they might *feel* that they could — especially if they'd had a few!).

Your own list of active words will be closely related to the things you have to do to prove that you know the subject well (whether to yourself, or to someone else — for example in a test or exam).

Section 6

HOW CAN YOU MAKE
BEST USE OF YOUR TUTOR?

(A tutor, if you've got one, is there to help you. Make sure he or she gets the chance.)

Not all open learning schemes use tutors. If you know that you won't have one on your programme, it may still be worth you going through this section. Partly to find out what a tutor does and what, therefore, you're missing. There are some ways of making up for the lack of a tutor.

Where tutors are used, their roles can vary a lot from one open learning programme to another. Some schemes use 'distant' tutors. There, the learner sends work to the tutor from time to time, often at times agreed between the two. Alternatively, some programmes of study have fixed 'cut-off' dates by which written assignments have to be in for marking. The Open University does this on most of its courses. (Of course, fixing the pace at which learners can work in this way is not really in the spirit of open learning, so in one respect at least the Open University is quite 'closed'!)

You may never see a tutor at all in some schemes, yet you may still send in assignments or tests to be marked by one. However, if you're in such a position, the chances are you'll get to know your tutor rather well through letters, comments on your work and telephone chats. I'm a distant tutor myself and I've got people still writing to me now and then who finished their courses with me years ago.

Many courses combine distant and face-to-face tutoring. There could be one person who marks assignments you send by post and another whom you see now and then. Maybe you'd meet as part of a small group in a local centre or college. Or maybe there'd be occasional residential course weeks or weekends where you could not only get some face-to-face contact but also 'hands-on' experience (for example using the new technologies, and so on).

Or again, your open learning programme could involve regular sessions in a centre. Then you'd probably have more than one tutor, maybe one in each of several subjects. In some open learning programmes in the new technologies (for example advanced electronics), tutors are technical experts from the industries involved.

So you see, there's no fixed job description of the open learning tutor. Like any other job, there are excellent tutors and bad ones, and all sorts in between. If you've got one (or more), you'll get to know which! Actually, the chances of getting a bad distant tutor are rather slim, partly because such tutors are not usually paid much and are not doing it for the money but because they enjoy tutoring.

SAQ 6

Imagine for a moment you'll be having a distant tutor. You've never met this tutor and maybe never will, you don't know yet. You have just finished your very first assignment and it is sealed in the envelope ready to be posted to your tutor for marking. Write a few words about how you expect you'll be feeling at that moment.

After jotting down your expected feelings above, please turn to the end of the section and compare what you've put with my comments there.

GETTING THAT FIRST ASSIGNMENT OFF!

You can guess from our exploration of feelings in SAQ 6 that many learners hesitate to post that first assignment. It may, if there isn't some sort of deadline for it, lie around for weeks till the courage is found to pop it in the post. Of course, your tutor can't help you with any problems you may be having until he or she knows what the problems are. So the sooner that assignment gets there, the better for both of you.

A first assignment is always a bit of a gamble anyway. You might have done much more than your tutor expects you to. It is possible, of course, that it's not up to the standard aimed for but, if so, you need to know this so that you'll be able to work towards such standards in future assignments. The only way you can find out is to send it in, preferably without waiting till you think you've got it as perfect as you can. However good it is, there will always be some things you haven't thought of.

You'll always be temped to hang on to the work because you'll know that, with a little more time and a little more effort, you could make it better. However, the chances are that you'll do better *faster* if you send it straight to your tutor who will quickly find where any difficulties are. This is often more efficient than hanging on, hoping to find and resolve all your problems yourself.

WHAT IF I'M REALLY STRUGGLING?

Usually, there's some sort of 'Help!' mechanism in an open learning scheme. Some schemes have 'hotlines' where, for stated hours of the day (or night), there'll be someone at the end of a phone line who will talk your problems over with you. That someone may not be able to answer any given problem there and then but he or she will most definitely be willing and able to direct your problem to someone who can really help you and that someone will get back to you as soon as possible.

Sometimes, you may be encouraged to make contact with your tutor even before sending any work in. You may have his (or her) phone number but feel frightened to ring up in case he is angry at being disturbed. However, if your tutor is the sort to get cross at an unexpected call for help from you, it's time he was no longer tutoring!

Even if he's just sat down to his dinner, he'll probably say 'I'm tied up for the next half-hour but can I have your phone number and I'll ring you back after then'. That means he pays most of the cost of your phone chat! If you're really too scared, you can, of course, write instead. In some ways, writing is actually better. You can take your time explaining your problem and your tutor can take his time deciding what advice or help will be most effective (and he gets his dinner in peace!).

All these worries will seem so trivial once you get to know a good tutor. He or she becomes much more a friend than a tutor.

YOUR ATTITUDES TO YOUR TUTOR'S COMMENTS?

Let's imagine that your first assignment has now come back to you. With racing pulse, you pick it up from the doormat and open it. What do you get? Your first impulse will be to look for your score or grade if it's an assignment that is being quantitatively assessed. If it's good, you'll feel great. There's no harm in that, of course. But if it's not so good, you could feel hurt, insulted or let down, certainly discouraged, even perhaps like giving up altogether. Many open learners do give up when this happens.

Don't be one of their number. Let me say one important thing in capital letters!

THE LEAST IMPORTANT THING ABOUT YOUR
ASSIGNMENT IS ITS GRADE OR SCORE.

What *is* important is the feedback you can gain by looking at your tutor's comments and explanations, and finding exactly what went wrong when errors happened. You can find out all sorts of things from a marked assignment. You can find things that you obviously did well enough and can build on these in the future. You can find things to avoid next time. You can learn from an experienced person's comments about ideas you included.

Now I know it's hard to take criticism, especially when you've tried your hardest already. A good tutor tries hard too and the criticism, if it's needed, will be of the constructive kind. Ideas that you can build on in the future will be given. So don't be defensive. Keep an open mind, willing to learn. Your tutor may not always be right, in fact. But even then, it's worth knowing that there's another view possible besides your own. Think of someone you know who always seems to see both sides of any problem. Yes, he's a pain in the neck if you're firmly on one of the sides! But such people are usually respected, they're 'wise'.

 **HELP YOUR TUTOR TO
HELP YOU**

How can you do this? Well, let's explore some possibilities.

Perhaps you haven't got deadlines. Maybe deadlines would be useful for you to pace yourself through your studies and build some sense of urgency into your work. *Ask* your tutor for some deadlines. Ask when you should send your next assignment in by. Ask when you should expect to be halfway through the course.

Perhaps you need extra help in identifying your strengths and weaknesses. How about this for an idea? In a covering letter with an assignment, what would happen if you said

> 'I reckon I'm good at . . . . but I'm struggling a bit with . . . . . Do I need to do a bit more work on . . . . ?'

Your tutor would be delighted and he'd be pleased to advise you. It helps your tutor to tell him what you think you're good at. Your tutor will even be pleased if you state directly

> 'I think the best way you could help me at the moment is if you were to . . . . '

If you find an area of work that you know is causing you problems, tell your tutor about them. Ask for some further practice questions; most tutors are delighted to spend a little extra time devising some extra work for a keen learner.

AND IF YOU HAVEN'T A TUTOR AT ALL?

For a start, you can use anyone to agree some deadlines with. You can use a friend or colleague to agree to be at the end of Module 5 by December 31st. Just the fact that you've taken someone into your confidence helps you pace yourself. In fact, you can make a sort of 'contract' with someone else to keep you to the straight and narrow. Such a person can ask you every now and then

> 'Well, how's the open learning going these days?'

You've then got to live up to his or her expectations which is usually more compelling than simply having to live up to yours.

You can get someone else to read things you've written. It doesn't have to be an expert. Just having another pair of eyes look at one's work always gives rewards — as long as you're not defensive or hostile to comments. You'll always learn something useful if you give yourself the chance.

> 'What do you honestly think of this?'

is all you need ask. If you get several people's views, all the better.

OBJECTIVES CHECKLIST

Now that we've looked at some aspects of a tutor's role in open learning, check that you are ready to:

(1) Regard your tutor as a helper rather than an assessor.

(2) Use your tutor to sort out the bits of the course that you don't understand properly.

(3) Use your tutor to keep you at it — or use other people if you haven't a tutor.

(4) Adapt your attitude to critical comment if necessary (and even say 'thanks' for it!).

ACTIVITY 6

Do this activity if you'll have a distant tutor — or even one that you'll occasionally meet.

Make a one-page summary of yourself to send to your tutor. This could include notes on:

> Factual details
> Name, address, work address, phone numbers, etc
> What you're studying at present
> What you may study next
> Why you're studying
> Approximately how many hours per week you intend to study on average
> What sorts of help you think you'll need
> Things you think you're already good at.

Plus anything else that you think will interest your tutor and help him to help you.

RESPONSE TO SAQ 6

A reminder of the question, first.

SAQ 6

Imagine for a moment you'll be having a distant tutor. You've never met this tutor and maybe never will, you don't know yet. You have just finished your very first assignment and it is sealed in the envelope ready to be posted to your tutor for marking. Write a few words about how you expect you'll be feeling at that moment.

RESPONSE

Here are some things that open learners have said about their feelings when sending off that first assignment to a distant tutor:

— glad it is done at last!
— apprehensive.
— excited.
— scared of what the tutor might say!
— impatient to find out how it measures up.
— fear of showing myself up.
— is it going to be tidy enough?
— is my spelling all right?
— exposed and vulnerable.
— is it good enough?
— will the tutor be critical?
— how quickly will I get it back?
— defensive.
— looking forward to being told how good it is.

Well, the chances are that the feelings you put down are there somewhere. If so, the main thing to notice is that you're not alone. You wouldn't be the first to be apprehensive, for example. In fact, that's a very common answer. It may be a natural feeling but there's really no need for it and a good tutor will soon be doing everything possible to put you at your ease.

Section 7

HOW CAN YOU REVISE PAINLESSLY?

(Organisation is a better painkiller than aspirin!)

It used to be called 'swotting' when I was at school! You know what I mean by 'swotting'? Of course you remember it. It also used to get called revision. In fact, most people still call it revision. I don't — at least I don't *think* of it as revision any more. Let me tell you why. The word revision means 'looking again', doesn't it? Well, by this time you should be convinced that just looking at something, however many times you do it, is not an efficient way of learning things.

It's all too possible to sit at your table or wherever, turning the page every few minutes. But after a while, if I came up and asked you 'Tell me all about the topic you were doing five pages ago', you may well have forgotten it again. In fact, you would have been wasting a lot of your time. You'd probably remember the *first* things you learned as you sat down and the *last* thing you read before I interrupted you but what about all the rest? Down the drain, maybe?

For reasons like this, 'revision' has a bad image in many minds. It's associated with long, boring times spent trying to cram knowledge into the memory. It's linked to deprivation — of the company of fellow human beings and of all the things you'd rather have been doing at the time. So let's get rid of the word and find something better, to fit a much more productive strategy than simply repeated

63

'looking again'. Please now cross out the word 'revision' below.

R E V I S I O N

Now, under the crossed-out word, write these words: *ACTIVE RECONSTRUCTION*. I agree it's a bit of a mouthful but it sounds much healthier, doesn't it? For a start, it implies something more active and less boring. 'Construction' is also a positive word, meaning building up things. Repetition is indeed essential if you're going to be able to remember how to build up your subject bits and pieces, so the word becomes 'reconstruction'. Right now, we've exorcised the ghost of that bad old word! However, we can't go through life saying 'active reconstruction' every time we would have used the word revision! So, let's make a compromise: let's *think* about active reconstruction every time we see or use the word revision! Now let's see what sort of a reviser you are.

SAQ 7

Which of the following most nearly fits you when it comes to learning your subject intensively, for example before an exam?

(a) I always leave it till the last minute — and wish I hadn't!

(b) I try to work for hours on end and often feel that my poor old brain just isn't taking things in.

(c) I practise systematically all the way through my studies and enjoy the feeling of always being on top of my work.

(d) I don't do any real swotting. I rely on having worked all the way through my course.

(e) I find all sorts of reasons *not to start* swotting!

(f) I revise in an organised, systematic way as the exam approaches.

(Your own patterns could involve more than one of these choices. Or, indeed, your own strategy could be different altogether. For the moment, however, go on to look at the responses I've made to each of the choices above, turning to the end of this section.)

WHAT'S THIS 'ACTIVE RECONSTRUCTION'?

Actually, it's just a commonsense extension of the ideas we looked at in Section 5 of this guide. Remember those learning tools we talked about? Question banks and summaries, in particular.

When you're preparing for an exam, what you're really preparing for is to be able to *do* things on command. If it's a written exam, you'll be answering questions, or drawing things, or interpreting things, and so on. If it's a practical test, you'll be doing things in a more physical sense. Remember all those 'active words' we talked about in Section 5? If you made a list of those words that apply to your particular subjects, those are the things that you need to prepare to do on command.

All these 'doing' words have one thing in common: the more often we 'do' whatever it is, the faster we get at it. Also, if we 'do' something several times, we're very likely to be able to do it anytime, including in an exam. Put it the other way round. Suppose you are sitting in an exam room and you see a question to which you know the answer but you've never actually answered it before, you've just *thought through* the answer. It will take you a lot longer to answer the question than it would if you'd written similar answers often before. It's as simple a principle as 'practice makes perfect'.

Suppose you were going to allocate an hour of your time to learn a particular bit of subject matter. Let's take two ways you could do it.

Way 1
Spend the whole hour going through it thoroughly and trying to get it to stay in the memory.

Jot down below any advantages and disadvantages of this 'Way' before looking at 'Way 2'.

Way 2

Day 1. Spend 10 minutes reading through the material, then 15 minutes reading through it more slowly, this time writing down short, sharp questions you would need to be able to answer about the bit of material concerned. Then stop.

Day 5. Spend 5 minutes with your list of questions from Day 1, finding out which ones you can still answer but, more important, identifying those where the answer has slipped from your mind since Day 1. Then spend 10 minutes with the original material, making a postcard-sized summary of the points which had slipped.

Day 11. Spend 10 minutes with your list of questions. *Think* through the answers to the ones you know you can do but *jot down* skeleton answers to the ones that slipped on Day 5, using your summary from that day as a last resort if you have to.

Day 15. Same as Day 11 but just 5 minutes (because less will have slipped this time).

Day 24. Another 5-minute check through that list of questions, with the odd minute used to polish up anything that is still managing to slip (but this isn't likely).

Total time in both 'Ways': 60 minutes.

Now, Way 2 is highly 'contrived' but deliberately so, for the sake of argument. Ask yourself this question now, then glance back at the 'Ways': 'Suppose there was a test on the topic on Day 35. Which 'Way' would work best?'

I think you'll agree that Way 2 would work best. If the test had been on Day 2, Way 1 would probably have worked well. But if the test was on Day 2, the test would probably include much more material than we were talking about learning in that hour, maybe 24 times as much. So you would then have to spend all 24 hours of Day 1 using Way 1. Using Way 2, on the other hand, you've plenty of time to apply a similar technique to all the other bits of subject matter. There's all those days we said nothing about between Day 1 and the test.

Now I'm not suggesting that you do your 'active reconstruction' in as rigid a manner as in 'Way 2' that I used to argue the case. It's the principle that is important, the principle of a little bit, often, with checks to make sure that it hasn't slipped every now and then.

CAN ANYONE HELP YOU WITH YOUR REVISION?

The old-fashioned revision used to be a very 'private' sort of activity. Do you remember? It would be done when you were on your own. You probably didn't want anyone to know you were doing it, in case they called you a swot or a stick-in-the-mud. Remember the loneliness of the long-period reviser? It needn't happen again!

For a start, you'll have guessed that I'm suggesting short spells, often, rather than long spells, occasionally. But what about the loneliness? Well, if you feel lonely working on your own, you're missing the company of people that you might be with if you weren't working. OK so far? Think now: would it be possible to *use some of these people to help you in your task*? Even just one person? Write down the name of someone who may be able to help you.

What could someone do to help anyway? Perhaps the person in mind doesn't know a thing about the subject you're learning. So what? He or she can still *ask you your questions*. This puts you on the spot. If someone else is asking you the question, you can't kid yourself 'Oh yes I'm sure I know how to do that one, let's move on' when in fact you don't know the answer. Your friend will be quick to spot when you try to waffle! Letting yourself be put on the spot like this is good practice for the real test that might be coming up. It's active reconstruction, isn't it?

If you let other people help you with your revision, there are more advantages. They'll help keep you at it.

> 'Isn't it about time you gave me another of those lists of questions to fire at you?'

> 'Remember that question that beat you yesterday? Can you answer it now? Go on then.'

And you're not as lonely as you would have been on your own. Would other people scoff at the idea of helping in such a way? It could happen but is not likely. You can tell from the reactions you get when you ask, who your *real* friends are.

Later, you could find yourself in the exam room confronted by a particular question. 'Ah yes, that's the one Jane kept bothering me with, I remember now' and on you'd go with your answer, thinking back to how you'd explained it to Jane.

ABANDONING THE HARD SLOG

From what we've explored already, you'll know that it's more fun to work in short bursts, working actively. There still could be times when you've got so much to do that, even though you're doing bits and pieces of this and that and giving yourself variety, you're still spending a lot of each day 'at it'. Is there a danger of this just becoming another kind of hard slog? Yes there is but you can avoid it by using a bit of discipline.

For a start, don't sit 'at it' for long spells of time. Anything over an hour may be far too long to maintain your efforts. You'd get very tired — after all we're talking about active reconstruction, not just easy reading. Take a break now and then. It need not be a long break. 15 minutes walking around or making some coffee can work wonders. Maybe you'll need a break after three-quarters of an hour. Maybe after half-an-hour. When you come back from a break, your efficiency will be restored. It might have declined a lot if you'd just carried on working.

Plan for yourself some time off! Deliberately plan to have the odd day off now and then, and the odd half-day off, and so on. If time off is part of your *plan*, you'll find that you can really relax and enjoy it. You'll enjoy it in a way you wouldn't have done if you'd slunk away from the work you felt you should have been doing. If you're getting really tired today but know that tomorrow is one of your planned days off, you'll find the energy to stick at it today.

Lastly, when doing a lot of active reconstruction, make sure that you use the advantages of giving yourself *variety*. Don't plod on and on with one troublesome topic. If something is causing problems, put a time limit on it, then go back to something more digestible. Go back to the troublesome bit for a while next day, when you're fresher. Eventually you'll crack it. Our minds don't grasp things in large chunks. They're magpie-like, they pick up a bit of this here, a bit of that there. *Make use of* this feature of how we learn. Deliberately do a bit of this now and a bit of something else later. With plenty of 'coming back and having another go', the bits and pieces will soon start to join together nicely.

OBJECTIVES CHECKLIST

After our exploration of revision, sorry *active reconstruction* strategy, do you now feel that:

(1) It's not just something that you should start towards the end of a course?

(2) It's best started by making learning tools (such as question banks and summaries) as a normal part of studying, right through the course?

(3) When an exam looms near, you now have nicer ways of working efficiently than the long, hard slog?

(4) Your strategy now focuses in directly on the 'slippable' stuff and makes sure that it doesn't slip when you need it?

ACTIVITY 7

A simple one but a useful one.

Make two little lists:

(1) Things I used to do when revising that I'm not going to do ever again!

(2) Things I am going to do in future which I didn't previously do when revising.

If you get friends to help you in some stages of your plans, it may be worth showing them these lists, they'll help to keep you to your intentions!

RESPONSES TO SAQ 7

First, the question once more.

SAQ 7
Which of the following most nearly fits you when it comes to learning your subject intensively, for example before an exam?

(a) I always leave it till the last minute — and wish I hadn't!

(b) I try to work for hours on end and often feel that my poor old brain just isn't taking things in.

(c) I practise systematically all the way through my studies and enjoy the feeling of always being on top of my work.

(d) I don't do any real swotting. I rely on having worked all the way through my course.

(e) I find all sorts of reasons *not to start* swotting!

(f) I revise in an organised, systematic way as the exam approaches.

RESPONSES

(a) If you always leave swotting to the last minute and then wish you'd done it earlier, you're in the same mess most people get themselves into! You'll certainly have painful memories of revision. You'll *know* within yourself that you should do something about that 'starting earlier' bit. But will you? Well, I think you might when you find out how to make the work involved more active, more enjoyable, more efficient and less time-consuming.

(b) No wonder your poor old brain feels that it isn't taking things in, if you've tried to force it to slog on for hours on end! You've been cruel to it. What's worse, you've been wasting a lot of the time you spent. You've been tiring yourself out pointlessly. You've probably been passive for most of those long hours. When you've tried the more active processes I suggest in this section, you'll find that your brain doesn't get that 'saturated' feeling.

(c) Are you *sure* that you can say you revise systematically all the way through your studies and so enjoy the feeling of always being on top of your work? I only ask because so few of us can honestly say that. Obviously, if you do this, that's splendid. I hope, though, that you'll find the ideas in this section can give you even greater satisfaction in your studies and maybe mean that you can take on more studying in a given time.

(d) You say you don't do any real swotting and rely on having worked all the way through your course. That's not quite the same as option (c) was. It's the systematic bit that's missing. It's one thing to have worked hard all the way through but another thing still to be able to do, at the end of the course, all the things you were happily doing at the beginning and in the middle. It would be no use only being able to answer exam questions on the last third of the course. Your maximum mark could be as low as 30%!

Even if you are on top of your studies, if you're going in for an exam, it's still worth doing a bit of special preparation — a bit of real practice that will speed up your performance in the exam, when speed does indeed matter.

(e)   You admit to finding all sorts of reasons not to get started with your swotting! Remember Sections 3 and 4 of this guide? All those possible reasons for not getting some real work done? What were they? *Excuses!*

Think about it now. Think of all the time you spent inventing those excuses! Think of all the days in your life you spent with a guilty conscience because you knew you should be doing something and you weren't doing it. Did you enjoy those days? Not as much as you would have if you'd done some work. In fact, you probably used up far more *energy* with your excuses and guilty conscience than it would have taken to make a big impact on getting some real work done.

(f)   Well done for revising in an organised, systematic way. Don't you find, though, that simply because the exam date is looming up, it's not so easy for you to learn things in a calm and thorough way? When you know there's plenty of time, it's easier to learn things. Also, there's more chance for practising skills. So I'm really suggesting that you keep up the 'organised, systematic' part of your method but start earlier, making revision a normal part of your work schedule, rather than a marathon effort towards the end.

Section 8

HOW CAN YOU GIVE OF YOUR BEST WHEN IT MATTERS?

(Or would you rather go to the dentist's than take an exam?)

WILL YOU HAVE EXAMS?

This section is about exams. I'm calling them exams but the things I want you to think about apply to all sorts of test — even the driving test! So if your open learning programme doesn't include any kind of formal assessment, I hope this section will still be of interest.

Many people *hate* exams! Probably most of us have had such feelings. Maybe we link exams to feelings of tension and anxiety. What if exams could be linked to feelings of confidence and delight at being able to prove that you know the subject well? I hope this section will help make your feelings about exams more positive.

Maybe you are studying something where it's entirely up to you whether you take an exam at the end of it. Let's say there is one you *could* take. But you haven't decided yet — it seems a long way off anyway, just now. It's worth tuning in your mind, even now, so that you'll prepare for that exam possibility (perhaps in a much more relaxed way than you've ever done before). The reason I'm suggesting this is that, as the exam date draws nearer, if you've been 'hiding it away', pretending it doesn't exist, it will suddenly seem frightening as it becomes closer. Then, you may go through all the negative emotions that so many suffer when coming up to exams. You might decide it would be easier to postpone it for another year or whatever. Then, having postponed the exam, 'why bother doing any studying? It's miles away', you may feel. See what a vicious circle that is.

The other possibility is the simple one: there *is* an exam and you are expected to take it. You need a good result from that exam. It's part of your plans. Let's see how you cope with exams.

 **SAQ 8**

Which of the following resembles most how you feel about exams at the moment?

(a) I'm scared stiff of exams!

(b) I never seem to do as well in an exam as I know I *could* have done, somehow.

(c) Exams don't bother me, in fact I quite like them.

(d) I think exams are an unfair way of measuring people.

(e) I usually do far better in exams than I really deserve!

How did you get on? We'll now go into a bit more detail of ways of making sure that you do yourself full justice in any exam you take in the future. We'll also see what we can do about any problems you've had in the past and try to make sure they don't bother you again! Probably the best way forward is if we go in sequence through good things to do before, during and even after your exam.

BEFORE AN EXAM

The things you do just before an exam — let's say during the 24 hours before it starts — can affect how you feel during the exam itself. How you feel at the very beginning of the exam can be affected quite a lot.

In particular, you don't want to be using up your reserves of mental energy (and even physical energy) on pointless tasks just before an exam. Here's a short list of pointless tasks. They can all be avoided by a bit of forethought!

Last minute searching for the exam room location.

Rushing to get there on time because you set out too late.

Scrabbling round looking for pens and pencils.

Hurrying to the shop to get a battery for the calculator.

No doubt you can add some of your own to this list!

It's best not to try to do too much last-minute revision. You need to save your energy for the exam questions. It's no use doing so much revision that during the exam you *know* it all but are simply too *tired* to get it down on paper!

Another thing to avoid is that little cluster outside the exam room before they let you in. Remember it? Here's what you hear:

'Do you know X?'
'Do you think we'll get a question on Y?'
'I found it hard to learn Z.'
'I hope they'll give us one on Q.'
'I hope they miss out W.'

As you stand there, what happens? You begin to think that everyone knows everything better than you do. Every time someone mentions a bit you haven't studied much, your feelings sink! And the tone's a bit like a racing commentary, getting more feverish as the start time gets closer. *Avoid it.*

75

THE FIRST TEN MINUTES

These are very special. They can be 'make or break' minutes. You may naturally be a bit tense as you prepare to see what's in store for you but it's now when you need to be your coolest. You've got some decisions to take. Actually, they're very easy decisions, if you approach it logically. You'd be surprised how many candidates (because that's what you're now called) make a mess of this simple bit of decision making. What decisions?

(1) HOW MANY QUESTIONS HAVE I TO DO?

(2) HOW MANY MINUTES FOR EACH QUESTION?

(3) WHICH QUESTIONS SHALL I DO (if there's a choice)?

The best thing you can do in these early minutes is slowly and carefully make these decisions. Work out an approximate timetable, splitting the available time up among the number of questions you have to try, leaving say a quarter of an hour 'spare' at the end — more about that later.

Then, for most of the first ten minutes, read each question very slowly, and more than once, before you decide whether it's one for you. If it's not, maybe put a cross beside it. If it's a 'possible', maybe a tick. If it's a 'definite', maybe two ticks beside it. After you've done this with all the questions, you'll know which is going to be your best one and it's good to start with that.

Plenty of candidates in past exams can tell you tales of how they missed their best questions by not reading the paper thoroughly enough at the start of the exam. If you follow my suggestions above, you'll not be joining them!

A final word of advice — even though it may seem very obvious to you. Check for those important letters 'PTO' at the foot of every page of the question paper! Sometimes candidates don't notice these letters and miss even seeing the questions on the next page. That next page may well have contained their best questions.

THE MAIN PART OF THE EXAM

When you are answering your best questions, the main danger is that you'll say too much because you know a lot about them. This is a serious danger because, if you do over-run, you may not have time for your last questions at all. If you were supposed to do five questions and you only did three, your maximum mark would be 60 per cent. And that would be if all your three answers were 20 out of 20! Now, if you do all five questions, you only have to score 12 out of 20 each time on average to get a total of 60 per cent. It's much easier this way.

Always show your 'working out' in any calculation-type question. If you just have a muddle of numbers down and you get the wrong answer, you can only get zero marks for that bit. You may only have made one simple mistake. But if the examiner can't see that you were correct most of the way, he can't give you any mark at all. Now if he *can* see where your mistake happened, he'll give you marks for the other correct things you did, so even with the wrong answer you could earn 19 out of 20, say. This means you could have lost 19 marks simply by not making it easy enough for the examiner to see what you were trying to do!

Ever had your memory go blank on you? Frightening when it happens. Actually, it doesn't just happen, you *made* it happen if you've suffered this. What you'd probably been doing is this: struggling to remember something that you knew *was* there somewhere but was lost for the moment. Now, the more we try to force our brains to do something, the more they rebel, even to the point of closing down temporarily! So if you feel those panic symptoms even just starting, slow down, take a deep breath, and relax. If you were trying to remember something and it's gone, *move on* to another question for a while. Given the chance, the 'missing' bit of information will come back, not long after you've 'taken the pressure off'.

It's important to *stick exactly to the question* all the time. We'd all love to show off our knowledge of various bits and pieces given half a chance sometimes. An exam is not the time to do this. If you start giving things the question doesn't *require*, you're simply wasting your time. The marks to be awarded go with the *required* information. It's well worth reading the question every now and then to make sure you're sticking to it. Don't just read it at the beginning, then never again — by the end of 30 minutes you could be answering a very different thing from the original question!

THE CLOSING FEW MINUTES

During the last quarter of an hour or so, even if you've still not finished some of the questions, it's worth stopping writing and starting this:

QUICKLY READ THROUGH ALL THAT YOU'VE DONE.

As you read you'll find:

Mistakes. Quickly amend them as you go. Often, you will find that what you have written down was not exactly what you *meant* to say. A few words here and there added in now can rectify that.

Bits you missed out, things that have come back into your mind since you wrote your answers: quickly slip them in.

Ways of 'tidying up' your script: underlining answers, main points, headings, ruling off between questions in sections.

If you use these closing minutes like this, it is possible that you could gain more marks in *this* quarter of an hour than in the preceding half hour! It's amazing how many candidates write down things that they would immediately have realised were wrong if they'd ever looked at the answers again. The examiner may even be able to tell that what was meant was different from what was written but he can't give marks for what he can guess, he can only give marks for what's there.

EXAMINERS ARE HUMAN!

Examiners *like* to be able to give out marks. They are just looking for things that earn the marks. The easier you make it for the examiner to find the mark-earning points in your answers, the happier he will be.

It is possible, however, to put an examiner in a bad mood! Going on and on about irrelevant things is one way! He's still got to read it all in case something relevant comes up but he'll get fed up with this. Also, if you've been writing so fast that your writing is illegible, it's harder work for the examiner. So sometimes it's worth saying that little bit less but writing it that little bit more neatly.

In most subjects, examiners *like diagrams*. Pictures, graphs and sketches tend to give a bit of visual relief to the examiner. Anyway, it's often quicker to explain something using a sketch rather than just in words. In such instances, the examiner may be able to tell more rapidly from your diagrams that you know something. As soon as he knows you know it, you've got your marks!

AFTER AN EXAM!

If you'll only have one exam, you can do whatever you like after it — I'm sure you'll know how to celebrate! What I'm thinking about is when you may have a group of exams. If you do the 'wrong' things after the first exam, say, it can demoralise you so much that you fail the second one, and so on.

What are the 'wrong' things? Well, what normally happens outside an exam room after it's over? What's it called? Yes, the *post-mortem*. It couldn't have a better name in fact. The exam is now dead! There's nothing at all you can do about it any more. So why *waste* your mental energy going over it all once again? Think of the chatter.

'Did you do question 5?'

'What did you get for the answer?'

'I didn't get that.'

'Did you remember to . . . . ?'

The more you listen, the more you feel that everyone else has done wonderfully and you've done terribly! By now, the people who actually *did* do well are probably doing something much more sensible.

What's the sensible alternative? Well, get away from that group for a start. Now you need a rest but probably need to wind down a bit before you can really relax. Have a go at this. Use some summary notes or question bank lists connected with your *next* exam for half an hour, *gently* doing a bit of revision for that. You may get the pleasantest of feelings: that of gently replacing all the information that was in your mind for the past exam with things you'll need for the next exam. After a little of this gentle revision, you'll be ready to have that rest. *And* you'll be much happier than if you'd done a post-mortem.

 **SUMMING UP**

Most of us left school with 'bad' feelings associated with exams. There used to be that mass-depression around, when they were on. Many of us didn't realise then that there's a lot of mileage in developing our skills in doing exams, not just trying to learn all of the subject matter. We can know it all very well and still not do ourselves justice in an exam.

It all comes back to practising the right things. All the way through this guide, I've been pointing out the advantages of *active* work.

Practising answering questions is particularly active and relevant to exams. It's that *active reconstruction* we were looking at in the previous section.

All you need to be able to do in an exam is the same sort of active reconstruction. The fact that you're sitting at a desk for a particular length of time doesn't matter. The fact that you're not allowed to speak doesn't matter. That you can't get up and make a cup of coffee every hour or so is a bit sad but you'll survive it. You can still take little bits of time off, sitting and daydreaming for five minutes just to give your brain time to gather its resources again.

And that fear of failure? If in the past you've ever failed an exam, do you now see that all that happened on that occasion was this (forgive me for repeating sentiments I gave in the response to SAQ 8(d) but I think it's important enough to need repeating):

on that particular day,
with those particular questions,
what you managed to write down
about what you knew
wasn't what was being looked for
by a particular fellow human
interpreting the questions in his way?

That's no disaster. If you've adopted the ideas I've been exploring with you, by the time your next exam comes you'll know the relevant things better, have had much more practice at answering questions, and have adopted a cool, logical approach to the matter of scoring the points in an exam. It's really a point-scoring game, after all.

If you get to regard exams as such a game, you'll get to like them more and more, until you actually enjoy them — challenges and all.

What more can I say about exams? Only that I hope the ideas in this section will help you to give of your best in them, whenever you need to. I hope also that you'll find you approach your next exam in good spirits. I'd also like to wish you the best of luck in your exams in future (though of course you won't *need* luck if you've done plenty of the right sort of preparation and if you adopt a logical, calm approach to tackling the exams).

OBJECTIVES CHECKLIST

Now that we've explored ideas about exam technique, do you feel convinced that:

(1) It's worth preparing for your exams all the way through your studies, not just towards the end?

(2) Making the learning tools we talked about in earlier sections of this guide is part of good preparation for exams?

(3) It's possible, and profitable, to be cool and well organised in those early 'decision-making' minutes of an exam?

(4) You can maintain a logical approach as you continue through the exam and avoid any bad things that happened to you in previous exams?

(5) You can use the closing minutes of an exam to pick up several extra marks which would have been lost if you'd just carried on writing, rather than spending a little time re-reading and amending?

(6) Examiners are human?

ACTIVITY 8

Here, I'm going to help you find out what it's like to be an examiner.

(1) Select an exam or assignment question on a topic you know well.

(2) Write out a model answer (you don't need to do this under exam conditions for this Activity), leaving a margin at the right-hand side of the paper.

(3) Now, suppose that your answer is a perfect one and is worth a full 20 marks. Take a red pen and decide what the mark-scoring points in your answer actually are (in other words, make a marking scheme for the question). Enter the marks scored in the right-hand margin.

(4) Use your tutor if you have one, or someone else who knows the topic if you've no tutor, as follows. Show him or her your answer and marking scheme, and ask whether you've missed out anything important from your answer and whether you seem to have divided the 20 marks sensibly.

RESPONSES TO SAQ 8

First, another look at the question.

SAQ 8

Which of the following resembles most how you feel about exams at the moment?

(a) I'm scared stiff of exams!

(b) I never seem to do as well in an exam as I know I *could* have done, somehow.

(c) Exams don't bother me, in fact I quite like them.

(d) I think exams are an unfair way of measuring people.

(e) I usually do far better in exams than I really deserve!

RESPONSES

(a) You admit to being scared stiff of exams! You're not alone! However, there's no need to be scared. Ask yourself these questions. Be honest:

Will your life be in danger?

Will you get injured or hurt?

Will you get insulted or harangued?

'That's all very well,' you're saying, 'but you don't know what I go through when I do an exam!' Well, another question:

What's the *worst* that could happen?

You may be thinking 'failure!' or various things. I trust that things I've explained in this section will convince you that your fears are unnecessary.

(b) So you don't think you're doing as well in exams as you could? This is often very true. The barrier between your present state and the happy state of getting full credit for everything you know may seem a big one but it's not. It's just a matter of skills. Skills need practice. A bit of practice along lines I suggest in this section should soon have you feeling much better equipped and ready to give of your best when it matters.

(c) Well done if you already quite like exams. I trust you'll bear with me for parts of this section when I offer advice to learners who have problems you've conquered. However, even if you like exams, it's always possible you could become even better at scoring the marks in them, so there should be something in this section for you too.

(d) So you think that exams are an unfair way of measuring people. Let's get one thing out of the way right now: exams *don't* measure *people*. You can't 'measure' a fellow human being! All an exam can do is measure this:

> What you can do
> on a particular day
> in whatever mood you happen to be in
> whatever your state of health
> with the particular tasks
> that someone happens to have devised
> for that particular exam
> your marks being judged
> by a particular fellow human
> in the mood he or she is in
> on another particular day, and so on.

Look at all the variables! It wouldn't be fair to measure anything with all these variables, you may think? Well, it's not so bad, as long as the *results* of exams are looked at with those variables still in mind. I agree with you that exam *results* are often taken far too seriously.

That said, the world we live in demands some sort of measure of what people can do and what they can't. So exam results get used but they are a very rough and ready measure after all and we're stuck with them as a measuring device.

(e) Well now, if you chose this option, you're saying you do better than you think you deserve to do in exams! Choosing this could mean several things, perhaps you know whether one of the following applies to you.

You've already got well-developed exam technique?

You're underestimating yourself?

Other people aren't as clever as they appear to be?

Anyway, use the advice in this section to make sure that it's not just due to good fortune that you've exceeded your expectations in exams in the past. Continue to exceed them!

SO, WHAT NEXT?

Well, as I've been saying so often, 'it's up to you!' But not quite yet. I'd like to leave you with one new thought. Here it is.

> 'Open learning is *not* just a poor substitute, to be used only when there is no conventional college course or training centre programme.'

Think back to things you've learned earlier in your life. The *teaching* may have taken place in classrooms, lecture halls, laboratories, training centres, and so on. But where did the real *learning* take place? My guess is that most real learning gets done outside the formal situations such as classrooms and so on. Most real learning is that which you did under your own steam. It's when you get your teeth into your notes, or your hands on the practical equipment, that the real learning starts.

Open learning programmes make the most of this. Materials are designed to help you learn under your own steam. So you're not using anything inferior when you use a good open learning programme. In fact, you're using a method which focuses on the way most real learning happens.

Finally, a last reminder that your responsibilities as an open learner include keeping your studying *active*. As I've explained in this guide, active studying should prove successful, efficient and, above all, enjoyable. Learning is a lifelong activity, so the time and energy you spend cultivating your learning skills along the lines I've suggested in this guide should be a sound investment in your future success. May I wish you every success with your studies.